AFFIRMED

BUILDING THE POSITIVE MENTAL HEALTH
OF YOUR PASTOR

DR. KIRK TRIPLETT

Affirmed: Building the Positive Mental Health of Your Pastor
Trilogy Christian Publishers
A Wholly Owned Subsidary of Trinity Broadcasting Network
2442 Michelle Drive
Tustin, CA 92780

10 9 8 7 6 5 4 3 2 1
Library of Congress Cataloging-in-Publication Data is available.
ISBN: 978-1-63769-762-7
ISBN: 978-1-63769-763-4

CONTENTS

PREFACE

Pastor Don was at the end of his rope. He was tired. Actually, he was exhausted. Gone were the days when he desired nothing more than to serve Jesus and share the love of God with others. He reminisced of the moment he felt the sacred call to help others. He remembered his days of study and preparation. He thought of the countless people who told them they were proud of him and that they were praying for him. Those recollections seemed a distant dream.

Don had grown to love the church. He loved the songs. He loved the fellowship. He even loved the potlucks (although he had learned to avoid certain dishes. Who ever thought tuna casserole was a good idea?) He loved the peace and the comfort that he found in the sanctuary. He loved God. He knew that God loved him, and he longed to share that love with others.

Now, years later, he sat in his office depressed, stressed, and wondering if God still loved him. He knew that God loved him, but he wrestled with feeling like a failure. The church members seemed to care more about the color of the carpet than reaching the lost. His elders felt distant and the ministry was overwhelming. Don wondered how people expected him to meet their needs when they never expressed those needs to him. He could not recall the last time he truly had a "day off," because church members would call or text him, even in the middle of the night with questions that seemed trivial and immature. Don sunk down into his chair, closed his eyes, and found...numbness.

If you are reading this as a pastor, you may relate to Pastor Don. If you are reading this as a church member, I hope you feel compassion for Pastor Don, and a desire to help. All too often, pastors feel these emotions, but are never expected to share these emotions. You see, pastors are supposed to have it all together. Oh, church members acknowledge that pastors are just human, sinners just like them, yet, they expect pastors to be different. After all, they only work on Sundays.

Pastors place a pressure upon themselves to be always ready and prepared. They never want to disappoint a parishioner and they desire to truly help and have answers for those with questions. Though they acknowledge that Jesus is the answer for every need, there is a pressure to be Jesus to others that often is overwhelming; a burden too great to carry.

PREFACE

You might be thinking, *What a depressing start to a book about positive mental health.* You might not be completely wrong in that thought. It is important to understand the struggles of pastors in order to understand how to help. My desire is that whoever reads this would seek ways to pray for the mental health of pastors and gain an awareness of the need. Additionally, my hope is that church members would seek ways to intentionally support the positive mental health of their pastors.

INTRODUCTION

"The WHO constitution states: "Health is a state of complete physical, mental and social well-being and not merely the absence of disease or infirmity." (https://www.who.int/news-room/fact-sheets/detail/mental-health-strengthening-our-response, 2021). This is different than the definition just fifteen years ago, where the WHO defined mental health as the "the absence of negative mental health and the components of mental illness." According to the WHO, until a decade ago, if a person suffered from depression, anxiety, stress, or any negative mental health emotion, that person was defined as having mental illness. With that definition, we all probably are mentally ill.

So, what does this have to do with pastors?

It should be noted that pastors are considered part of the helping professions. The professions are nurses, first responders, counselors, and pastors. Counselors have the worst mental health, and pastors are a close second. Why? I like to think of this as collateral damage of the profession. You see, when people come in and visit with a pastor they spiritually and emotionally vomit all over the office. Additionally, pastors typically find themselves always giving. After all, according to the Apostle Paul, Jesus said "it is more blessed to give than to receive."". (Acts 20:35, ESV)

Pastors find that the romance of ministry quickly fades, and they are faced with the reality that their work is often exhausting and thankless. Consider the fact that though office hours are posted, the expectation is that the pastor would be available whenever crisis arises. Church members often take advantage of the fact that the pastor tells them to "call anytime" as they are given his personal cell number. In an effort to be relatable, pastors' "Friend" everyone they can on Facebook and follow church members on Instagram (this is a great way for pastors to spy on parishioners and determine the next sermon series...☺).

Pastors typically do not join the ministry because all the cool kids or doing it or the financial benefits are so great, they could not resist. Most pastors will explain that they have a divine call from God to serve the people of God. It is sacred work. Although this is the driving force for many, church member impact the way a pastor feels about his calling. Many times, pastors begin to question their calling and whether or not they responded correctly to God when times, seasons, and attitudes of church members are negative.

Research groups have studied the reasons that pastor leave the ministry and church members lead the list. According to a The Fuller Institute, George Barna, and Pastoral Care Inc., "the number one reason pastors leave the ministry - Church people are not willing to go the same direction and goal of the pastor. Pastor's believe God wants them to go in one direction, but the people are not willing to follow or change (Maxwell, 2019). Church members matter.

The goal of this book is to take the results of my study on how pastors describe the way their positive mental health is influenced by the action of church members and help create an awareness to the real problem in churches with the tools to fix it. You see, what church members do matter, but too often they do not understand that what they do contributes to the mental health of their pastor. My hope is that whoever reads this book would take the information in the book and be part of the solution, taking what they have learned and strengthen the church by building their pastors' positive mental health.

CHAPTER 1:

BURNOUT IS SNEAKY

It is necessary to take a brief moment and explain why pastors find themselves frustrated, depressed, and considering leaving the ministry. This does not happen in an instant nor overnight. It is a process that occurs over time and often pastors are unaware that it is even present. Awareness is the key to change; both pastors and church members need to be aware of the factors that contribute to burnout.

Dr. Christina Maslach created the Maslach Burnout Inventory in 1986. The components of burnout were established by Maslach et al. (1986) when the Maslach Burnout Inventory (MBI) was created. The components of burnout are emotional exhaustion (EE), depersonalization (DP), and personal accomplishment (PA) (Salwen et al., 2017). Emotional exhaustion is concerned with the fatigue, depersonalization is also called cynicism, and describes disinterest or a distance in attitude, and personal accomplishment or personal efficacy, pertains to social and professional accomplishment (Portoghese et al., 2018).

Francis and Crea (2018) explain the use of the MBI to determine levels of emotional exhaustion, depersonalization, and personal accomplishment, all indicators of burnout, all contributors of NMH. However, Francis and Crea (2018) chose to curtail a burnout inventory that focused on the unique burnout aspects common among clergy. The criticism of the MBI stemmed from the sequential progression of burnout which began with emotional exhaustion which leads to depersonalization, resulting in low personal accomplishment (Francis et al., 2017). The Francis Burnout Inventory (FBI) was developed to assess the negative and positive effects in ministry (Francis, Village, Bruce, & Woolever, 2015). This was determined using the Scale of Emotional Exhaustion in Ministry (SEEM) for the negative effect and the Satisfaction in Ministry Scale (SIMS) for the positive effect (Francis et al., 2015).

Combatting NMH has been the topic of many studies over the years (Proeschold-Bell et al., 2016). These studies have led to various programs, including PMH strategies, to aide in the recovery and prevention of NMH. The need for PMH as a fundamental component to society, families, and individual well-being is clear (Vaingankar et al., 2016). Vaingankar et al. (2016) noted the growing evidence that PMH aides in combatting NMH and contributes to over-coming mental illness. Lluch-Canut et al. (2013) recog-nized the shift to looking for PMH started in the mid-20th century. It is important to note that a single criterion can-not determine or define PMH (Lluch-Canut et al., 2013). Cowen and Kilmer (2002) studied and listed sixty variables that contribute to PMH. In 1999, Lluch created a model for PMH that consisted of six factors: interpersonal relation-ship skills, self-actualization and problem solving, auton-omy, self-control, prosocial attitude, and personal satisfac-tion (Lluch-Canut et al., 2013).

Pastors are the leaders of many church organizations. Engelberg et al. (2016) addressed the church as an orga-nization and acknowledged that church having leadership styles and marketing as components to the church. Lau (2018) explained that the church is a unique organization, employing clergy to function as administrator, teacher, pastor, preacher, organizer, and leader. MacIlvaine III et al. (2016) explained that pastors are leaders within the church organization with the expectation of serving others in greater ways than other organizational leaders. Miner et al. (2015) expressed concern for the mental health of pastors and the impact the church leader has on the mental health of the organization. The mental state of the pastor influences their ability to lead effectively and teach positive mental health practices by example, thus impacting the mental state of the members of the church who seek the pastor for guidance (MacIlvaine III et al., 2016).

Research has noted that clergy can be surrounded by people constantly yet can feel socially isolated (Proeschold-Bell & Byassee, 2018). The pressures of pastors and their families are evident. Clergy and their families are challenged with role ambiguity, personal criticism, a lack of clear boundaries, presumptive and subjective expectations (Adams et al., 2017). As Proeschold-Bell and Byassee (2018) mentioned, tension arises from congregants disagreeing on how a pastor should spend his or her time. This tension can influence how a pastor assesses personal accomplishment.

Success for a pastor can be difficult to measure (Brewer, 2016) which contributes to the mental health of the pastor. The fact that spiritual growth in individuals is often not outwardly evident can cause pastors to question their effectiveness (Adams et al., 2017). Miner et al. (2015) realized the lack of research addressing indicators that contribute to church leader PMH. Some research has indicated that pastors with PMH have stronger personal relationships of support and friendship with church members than pastors with NMH (Proeschold-Bell & Byassee, 2018).

Though this is all technical, it is necessary to establish the reality that researchers have been studying and confirming the fact that burnout among pastors is a fact and something that should cause concern. Vaingankar et al. (2016) noted the growing evidence that PMH aides in combatting NMH and contributes to overcoming mental illness. If positive mental health combats negative mental health, then strategies can be formed to promote success. The following chapters will follow Pastor Don as he recalls the moments where the PMH components were used in his life, invigorating his drive for the ministry.

CHAPTER 2:

PERSONAL SATISFACTION

(LIFE'S SO, SO, GOOD)

What does it mean to be satisfied? Where do pastors discover personal satisfaction? Does satisfaction come from work or home? The answer is not simple. Personal satisfaction is how one looks at life with optimism and interpersonal relationship skills consisting of empathy and the ability to help others maintain positive relationships (Lluch-Canut et al., 2013). Not only does one look with optimism in life but they also encourage others to see the bright side of circumstances. Pastors feel personally satisfied with life and optimistic about the future when church members do certain actions.

Affirmation

Let's get back to Pastor Don. As Don sat slumped in his office chair, he asked for help. Whether he felt God was listening or not, he knew that only God could meet his need. In silence, he waited. Psalm 46:10 came to mind: "Be still and know that I am God," and all Don could think of was that he was numb, beyond still. Yet, he sat and waited. He remembered a moment in the past when he felt good about his calling and his ministry.

It was a time that pastors are invited into. These intimate moments of people's lives. Agnes was dying. She had lived a long life but was now nearing the end. She was on hospice and through the course of Pastor Don's visits, he asked if she had been baptized. She explained that she had been in the church when she was younger but hadn't been since she was eight or nine years old. She asked Pastor Don if she could be baptized. Don went to get some water from the kitchen and baptize her right then and there. Agnes refused and requested that she be baptized at the church. The next day, her husband brought her to the church and he and Don carried her up to the baptismal font. Don had offered to baptize her on Sunday, but Agnes did not have the strength to deal with all the people that would be there. She stood shaking and unstable at the baptismal font and Don baptized her. Don recalled a complete change in her countenance. He could tell that she was at peace. The next day, Agnes went home to be with the Lord.

It is moments like this that pastors feel affirmed in their ministry. When people respond to the work of the pastor in a positive way, the pastor knows they do not labor in vain. Affirmation appears in many different ways. It can be as simple as a church member coming to service more consistently, or the church member that responds to the sermon with enthusiasm. When a pastor knows that someone has their back and will support them, they feel affirmed. It could be as simple as an email or a note that expresses how important the pastor is to the church member. These simple moments affirm the pastor in his calling and helps them serve the church in more positive ways.

Thoughts began to flood into Pastor Don of moment after moment where he was affirmed in his work. He remembered Jack coming to him with tears in his eyes and expressing that no one had ever loved him the way Pastor Don had. He recalled Damon, who had come sparingly the first year Don was at the church, but two years ago started coming more frequently and signed up for the new member class. Then there was Sara, who came up to Pastor Don at the end of the new member class and asked to be baptized.

He remembered Joe, who had been away from church for years, but returned because of a moment he met Joe at the grocery store. These moments affirmed Pastor Don that he was doing a good job.

It doesn't take much for church members to affirm their pastor's calling and work. The challenge is that most church members do not consider how they might affirm their pastor. What if you looked for ways to give your pastor a boost and affirm, they are doing a good job? It begins by desiring that your pastor be as effective and impactful as possible. It means that maybe you need to consider his needs.

PERSONAL SATISFACTION

Questions to consider:

How will you affirm your pastor this week?

What specifically can you do to let your pastor know they are fulfilling their calling?

Challenge: Intentionally pray for your pastor every day.

Engagement

Pastor Don breathed a sigh and wiped the tears from his eyes. Was the recollection of these moments, God meeting him in his moment of trial? Still unable to move, Don began to think of Marci, a single mother with two young boys. These boys were filled with energy and passion, causing chaos. The chaos was compounded by Marci working a full-time job and a divorce that left the boys torn between their mom and dad. Don suggested that Marci make a point to sit down to dinner, with her boys, every evening, pray, read a Bible verse, and talk about the day. He warned Marci that it would be a difficult task, but one way that would help. As Marci left, Don was not optimistic that she would take his suggestion.

The next week Marci came in with excitement and gratitude. She had taken Pastor Don's advice and planned the week of dinners. She told her boys that this evening connection at dinner time was non-negotiable. She admitted the first couple of nights were challenging but noticed that by the end of the week the boys were beginning to calm down and engage in conversation. In fact, they seemed to be calmer throughout the week and more respectful of their mother.

PERSONAL SATISFACTION

Pastors are always asked how to deal with circumstances and situations in life, however, most often church members disregard the suggestions. There are various reasons why church members do not take the advice of the pastor. Too often people are looking for the quick fix and pastors offer altering your lifestyle and denying yourself. This idea of considering others and living the Christian life is often rejected and pastors are left with wondering why they were approached by the church member in the first place.

Each week sermons are given. Each week people come and listen. It is important to understand that pastors are not interested in church members hearing a good story or feeling better about themselves. The purpose of the sermon is to encourage people and equip them for the work of the ministry. This means that sermons are crafted to inspire change. Ephesians 4:11-12 (ESV) explains that Jesus "gave the apostles, the prophets, the evangelists, the shepherds and teachers, to equip the saints for the work of ministry, for building up the body of Christ." Pastors find great personal satisfaction when church members are engaged in the sermons and allow the Holy Spirit to use the sermons to increase their faith and influence Christian character in their lives.

Pastor Don found himself immersed in memories. Memories of times when he was excited about what God was doing. Times when he expected the unexpected because people were investing in others. The church was growing, not just numerically, but you could feel the energy that God was real to the church members. So real was God, that people were inviting others to church, parents were bringing their kids to Sunday school and youth group. The church longed to gather, and the fellowship was joyful and filled with laughter. Patrick, who had only been attending for less than a year, continually brought ideas of how to engage with the community and use the church as a station for community events. The future was bright. Don was excited. He realized that Patrick was still making suggestions and that the fellowship was sweeter as people were sharing life with one another and inviting others to join in the journey of faith.

It is important to understand that the work that pastors engage in is met with resistance. You see, life in Christ is more than a social club that meets once a week. Life in Christ brings you into a community of believers that are now charged, dare I say commanded, to reach out and bring others to Christ. Too often, church members are apathetic in their faith. Church members believe that it is the pastor's responsibility to share the gospel, and it is. However, the charge to preach the gospel extends to every believer, to every person who claims they are believers in Jesus.

Jesus commanded, "Go therefore and make disciples of all nations, baptizing them in the name of the Father and of the Son and of the Holy Spirit, teaching them to observe all that I have commanded you" (Matthew 28:19-20, ESV).

It is the call to every believer, to plead with others to respond to the conviction of the Holy Spirit and receive the free gift of salvation through faith in Jesus Christ. Pastors are optimistic about the future when the see church members understand that the Great Commission is not just for the first disciples or pastors, it is actually a call to every believer. Optimism comes when people share their faith and respond to the work of the Holy Spirit.

Some questions to consider:

How do you respond to the advice and the sermons your pastor gives?

What keeps you from valuing the words that your pastor offers?

Challenge: Tell your pastor what they have said or suggested that has impacted your life and your walk with Christ.

Optimism

Pastor Don wiped the tears from his eyes and began to think of the future. For some time now, he had been discouraged about the future and considered the upcoming days as bleak and hopeless. Then the thought of Barry, a single father, who approached him and asked that Don take his daughters through first communion. This meant that they would spend the next four weeks, with their father, studying God's word and seeing the importance of the Christian life. Don was surprised by Barry's ask, but immediately scheduled Monday afternoons to begin the classes. This made Don have a sense that the future is brighter because unexpected parents, like Barry, were responding to the Holy Spirit and desiring their children to follow the faith.

Pastors desire that the kingdom of God grows and that happens at the local church. It is more than church attendance, financial support, … it is commitment. But not just commitment to showing up regularly. No, it is called engagement. Though pastors love to see you every week, the love more to see you care about the work of the church which extends beyond the four walls. Engagement causes optimism, which gives pastors increased satisfaction in life.

The sacred call of the ministry is to "go and make disciples…baptizing…and teaching." But it is difficult when church members do not respond to the efforts of the pastor to teach them to obey all that Jesus taught.

If we could be honest, pastors like Sunday mornings, but they love the engagement throughout the week. When people bring their kids to youth group; when people engage in mid-week home fellowships or Bible studies; when people hang out after church and fellowship; when people invite friends, family, and coworkers to church; these are the things that give the greatest satisfaction to pastors. Too often, pastors wonder why church members come to church at all because it doesn't seem to impact their daily lives.

The Apostle Paul explains to the Corinthian church that they are "ambassadors" of the gospel. As you read, hear what God is saying through the Apostle Paul:

> Therefore, if anyone is in Christ, he is a new
> creation. The old has passed away; behold,
> the new has come. All this is from God, who
> through Christ reconciled us to himself and
> gave us the ministry of reconciliation; that is, in
> Christ God was reconciling the world to him-
> self, not counting their trespasses against them,

and entrusting to us the message of reconcilia-
tion. Therefore, we are ambassadors for Christ,
God making his appeal through us. We implore
you on behalf of Christ, be reconciled to God.

2 Corinthians 5:17-20 (ESV).

This is why pastors labor: To bring people to the saving
knowledge of Jesus Christ; equip them for the work of the
ministry; the ministry of proclaiming the good news of Jesus Christ; and sending them out week after week prepared
to impact their sphere of influence for the Kingdom of God.

So, how can you help your pastor have personal satisfaction in their life? Get involved. Grow in your faith. Respond
in the strength of the Holy Spirit and live the life that Jesus
is calling you to live. Be engaged. Find ways to serve at the
church. Ask the pastor how you can help. Make sure your kids
are at church. Esteem the gathering of believers above your
hobbies or your kids sports schedule. Come to church with
an expectation to hear from the Lord and act upon what he
says. Get connected in Bible study and midweek fellowships.
It seems difficult, and pastors never want people to feel that
they are obligated to participate in Christian activity, however,
the challenge to grow in your faith and take your eternal life
seriously is before you.

AFFIRMED

Some questions to consider:

How is God asking me to get more involved?

Why have you not participated in certain activities of the church?

Challenge: Get involved. Stretch yourself and find ways to plug in. Make the plan for more than one time but actually commit to the Lord and ask the Spirit to help you prioritize church engagement.

CHAPTER 3:

PROSOCIAL ATTITUDE

(I LIKE EVERYBODY AND THEY LIKE ME)

Most people think that pastors are social beings. After all, pastors engage in conversation every Sunday and seem to be extroverts that love everyone. The pastor commands attention. The pastor is the life of the party. He is a social butterfly. He seems to genuinely be interested in each person the talk with. They love being with people of all types. Right?

Prosocial Attitude addresses how one genuinely shows concern for the well-being of others. It includes how a pastor looks for ways that church members have helped them accept others and embrace differing social characteristics of people. Isn't it the pastor's job to lead by example and show that God loves everyone equally? Prosocial Attitude asks the question of how a person relates to people different than themselves.

This question can cause some challenges for those in pastoral ministry because it asks you to consider when you have helped someone of a different social status than yourself. Pastors consider their work sacred and one of the principles of the faith is to "let each of you look not only to his own interests, but also to the interests of others" (Philippians 2:4, ESV) and "not to think of himself more highly than he ought to think (Romans 12:3, ESV). The principle of serving others makes it challenging for pastors to view others as different. However, we cannot escape the fact that pastors often find themselves helping and working with people that are at a different place in life and in need of help.

Friendship

The phone buzzed with a text alert. Through watered eyes, Pastor Don looked at his phone. His friend, James, was inviting him to lunch. This made Don cry a bit more as he reminisced about how he and James met. James had walked into the church beaten down by life and nearing the end of his rope. He had relocated to the area to start again. James had experience hardship, but a new job opportunity brought him hope and a chance to relocate. Things were going well for James until the business had closed and he was out of a job. Desperately, James sheepishly walked into the church one Sunday morning. After service Don and James sat and talked. Immediately, there was a connection and Don asked how he could help James.

Pastors are not immune to the trials of the world. In fact, may pastors have shared experiences and can relate to the frustrations and disappointment of life. Though pastors preach hope and joy, it is always presented as a contrast to what we experience in life. Without the trials of life our joy is minimal. When pastors are invited into the moments of trial in a person's life, they find joy in laboring alongside another and helping. Many times, the unexpected outcome is a friendship that begins. When a pastor treats others as valuable, that person feels connected to the pastor because they were accepted in a moment of vulnerability and failure.

The phone buzzed again. James was surprised that Don had not responded yet. The invitation was extended again. Don picked up the phone and replied "I needed to hear from you today. Thank you. And yes!" James replied quickly with a thumbs up and a taco emoji. Don knew they were going to have lunch at the place that has the best street tacos, a guilty pleasure that he and James share.

One of the factors that pastors deal with is isolation. Many people find it difficult to connect with a pastor because they have set the pastor on a pedestal. Or church members don't think the pastor understands life in their world. Pastors desire to be with people in all aspects of life. Most pastors desire to be friends with others and provide a relationship that is built on trust and mutual value. This value is not just centered on a shared belief but on the value placed in each other.

That first Sunday, Don took James to have some street tacos. Don wondered if the tacos were really that good or if the place reminded them of the beginning of their friendship. It really didn't matter, what mattered was God had brought them together. James had physical needs and his spiritual and emotional exceeding the physical. Don provided both for James. After lunch, Don bought some groceries for James and invited him to start coming to the church weekly to hang out. As Don left James, he didn't think that James would show up. He was wrong. For two months James came every Tuesday and shared life with Don. James found a job and their weekly meetings moved from Tuesday afternoons to Saturday mornings. Though James acknowledged and knew that Don was his pastor, he was more, he was a friend.

There are many phone calls and meetings between pastors and people in need. Many pastors find the physical provision for people easy but exhausting. When Jesus fed the 5,000, He received and increase following of people wanting the free meals. Then Jesus changed the conversation and challenged the people to consider eternal food rather than the temporal needs of this world. Jesus explained that it was necessary to eat of His flesh and drink of His blood to have any relationship with Him. He knew the true need of the people was to be forgiven and find life in Him, yet this was not what many wanted. "After this many of his disciples turned back and no longer walked with him" (John 6:66, ESV).

Giving food, paying a utility bill, helping with rent, buying gas, and more, are all tasks that pastors participate in. However, a pastor did not enter the ministry to be a glorified social worker. He knows the real need for everyone is spiritual and he knows that the temporal, physical needs blur one's ability to see their need. Physical provision is great; spiritual awakening is better.

Some questions to consider:

Do you see your pastor as a friend? If not, why not?

What ways has your pastor made you feel lifted up and valued?

Challenge: Consider ways to let your pastor know that you value them as a person and not only a pastor.

Genuine Care

Pastor Don took a deep breath. Feeling a little more encouraged, he sat up in his chair and looked at the card that he had attached to the wall four years ago. Carol was fighting cancer and Pastor Don visited here during her chemotherapy treatment to encourage her and her husband Jacob. She was in remission and that card on the wall reminded Don that he was effective during Carol's season of need. What was more important were the specific words that were contained in the card. "Pastor Don, thank you for bringing Jesus to us and walking alongside us in our time of greatest need. Your presence and the words you always shared, brought us comfort and peace. The Holy Spirit used you then and continues to use you now. We thank God for you every day and pray for you. Though it's not much, please accept this gift as a small token of our gratitude." Don enjoyed golf. Golf is expensive. One of the days that he was visiting Carol during treatment, he was sharing his enjoyment of golf. Carol's husband asked him how often Don played. "Not that much," Don replied, explaining it was cost prohibited. Included in the card for ten rounds of golf.

Acts of genuine care bring greater joy to pastors, and

they are more likely to actively be social when they know members truly care for them. Though pastors receive smiles and thanks week in and week out, they find great satisfaction when they know that a church member cares enough to listen to who the pastor is as a person. It is never inappropriate to give genuine care to your pastor. The job of the pastor requires a lot of giving; giving of emotions, time, and energy. Caring for your pastor is one of the best ways you can ensure he will be built up and serve you and others well.

A few years ago, Pastor Don was coming down with a cold. He was outside after service chatting with several people. He explained that he usually didn't go to the doctor because when he felt a little under the weather, he would take Vitamin C, and Echinacea with Golden Seal. During the course of the informal conversation, Don mentioned that he was unable to find Echinacea with Golden Seal, and it seemed to be the supplement that boosted his immune system and was concerned that he could not find it. A couple of days later, Don walked into his office and there were four large bottles of Echinacea with Golden Seal on his desk.

When the pastor receives care that is specific and

intentional, they are lifted up and know that people are listening and attentive to their needs. Again, the goal is to work together, congregation and pastor, to build a strong and healthy body of Christ. As pastors pour into others, the Holy Spirit uses others to pour into the pastor. As pastors labor, it is important to let them know that their labor is not in vain. It doesn't take much. Pastors just want to know that they are loved and that they are helping those they serve.

Questions to consider:

How well do you know your pastor?

What keeps you from knowing the pastor?

Challenge: Think of a way you can bless the pastor this week with something intentional and thoughtful.

Gratitude

"Pastor Don, I want to thank you for how you explained that Bible verse in class this morning. I had always wondered about it and now I understand, and it really helps my walk with the Lord." These words were strength for Don's soul. All the years in college and studying week in and week out, actually paid off. Don recalled the comment he received wondering how he could remember all the facts and Bible verses. It wasn't that Don wanted to show off, but Don wanted to help others understand how verses connect to one another and how the Bible has been relevant and engaging at every moment in history. It was as if the Holy Spirit was speaking words of affirmation over Don.

Most pastors don't enter the ministry because it seemed like a good idea or something else didn't pan out for their career. Pastors want to be ready to help and have the answers that are found in the inspired, inerrant, Word of God. It is the longing of pastors that people would grow in their faith and believe like Peter "Lord, to whom shall we go? You have the words of eternal life, and we have believed, and have come to know, that you are the Holy One of God" (John 6:68-69, ESV). When church members respond to the

Word of God as presented by the pastor, the pastor knows they have invested in eternal work.

As Pastor Don was feeling refreshed, he opened up his email. There was a message from Jerry. Jerry had been attending the church for about two years. The last eight months, Jerry seemed to be more consistent in his attendance. Jerry would sit with a stoic look on his face and Don always wondered if Jerry was pondering the messages or if he was disinterested. As he opened the email, Don took a deep breath and then surprise lifted his spirit. "Pastor, I just wanted you to know that I have been listening to you for the past couple of years and it wasn't until yesterday, when you explained that we come to church to be equipped so that we can go out and do the work of the ministry, that I understood why I was coming week after week. I have never taken responsibility to share my faith because I thought that it was your job, but after Sunday's message, I recognized that I come to church so that I can learn how to share with others. The people I get to see at work and in my community aren't coming and listening to you every week, so I get to share with them. So, thank you. Also, I invited my neighbors to church, and I think they will be there Sunday. Feeling blessed, Jerry." What a joy Don was feeling.

He couldn't wait to see Jerry next Sunday and tell him how excited he was and to encourage him.

When a pastor is encouraged, they encourage others. Saying thank you is great, and pastors do appreciate it, however, when a person expresses how the words of the pastor encouraged their walk with the Lord, it is much more meaningful and impactful to the positive mental health of the pastor. The challenge is whether or not people attend church with the expectation to grow and change. If people attend for a social club or out of obligation, they will often be found wanting. However, when people attend church expecting to hear from God through the pastor, they participate in the work of the church and are able to specifically express gratitude to their pastor.

Questions to consider:

Why do you come to church?

What are your expectations when you arrive to worship?

Challenge: Pray that you would come with expectation to church and share with the pastor what happened at church that was beneficial.

CHAPTER 4:

SELF-CONTROL

(I'M FORCING THIS SMILE)

You might be thinking, *What does self-control have to do with positive mental health?* Well, when someone can exhibit their ability to regulate their emotions, they can be better at dealing with conflict and stress. Pastors have a stressful job that is often met with contention and dissention. When church members help pastors deal with conflict and stress, the pastor can combat the negative mental health components of stress, anxiety, and depression.

Stress Relief

Pastor Don began to thank the Lord for carrying him through a season of immense stress. The church was growing and the need to move to multiple services was before them. The church board was divided on how to move forward. Some were adamantly against two services but offered no solution. Others on the board proposed removing pews, replacing them with chairs. One person even suggested removing the wall between the sanctuary and the adjoining fellowship hall which was serving as an overflow room. Pastor Don suggested building a new building. This suggestion was met with great disagreement. Before the meeting was over, one board member had resigned in protest to the church growing.

You need to understand, no pastor joined the ministry to maintain a certain number of church members. All pastors desire to see the kingdom of God grow and when the enemy uses division in the church, pastors can feel defeated and discouraged. There will always be a part of the church that resists change. I mean, the world is changing enough, why should the church change. The church always, from generation to generation, has sought ways to introduce Jesus to others. This happens through change.

As Don walked to his car, he felt dejected and frustrated. Why was there resistance to growth? Why would someone leave the board in frustration? After all, the need to accommodate more people was a great problem to have. A notification rang on his phone. "Pastor, I wanted you to know that Janet and I love you and we do not feel you were treated right. You are doing a great job. Keep it up." Rob and his wife Janet were a constant source of encouragement. They always wanted Don to know that they had his back.

It is important to know that pastors need to know that people are on their side. This is especially true in stressful moments and times. When the church is functioning properly, and people are following the Holy Spirit, tensions and stress will come. Let's be real, even when the church is now growing or functioning well, there will be stress because people are present.

Questions to Consider:

When have you seen your pastor dealing with stress?

How can you be more aware of how stressful your pastor's work is?

Challenge: Reach out to your pastor and ask them how they are doing and is there any way they can help relieve any current stress.

Conflict Relief

"I can't believe that you are siding with him!" screamed
Darrell. It had been an intense meeting between Darrell
and Frank. They were church members that had gone into
business together and had an opportunity to expand but
there was a question of integrity. At one point, Pastor Don
thought he was going to have to break up a fight. Frank was
hesitant because he felt that the risk to expand was requir-
ing them to compromise their business principles based on
their Christian faith. "Whoever walks in integrity walks
securely, but he who makes his ways crooked will be found
out" (Proverbs 10:9, ESV) quoted Don. This was what had
set Darrell off.

Honestly, the construction business was not something
that Don knew. In fact, he was always designated to keep
others hydrated as they worked on construction projects
at the church. Once Darrell and Frank calmed down, Don
picked up the phone and called Allen. Allen was a board
member of the church and a businessman. He had been
successful and his reputation in the community and at the
church was exemplary. Allen had offered his ability and his
expertise in conflict relief to Pastor Don. Now that Allen

was willing to meet on the business, Don was able to calmly discuss the friendship and the brotherly love between Darrell and Frank. As Darrel and Frank left the office, Don expelled a big sigh of relief. He was thankful that Allen was in his life and willing to help. He was also thankful that Darrell and Frank were willing to reasonably work toward protecting their friendship.

Reasonableness, though subjective, indicates a willingness to listen and hold emotion at bay. Pastors often find themselves in the middle of emotional conflict. Marriage counseling and relationship strife consume much of a pastor's time. Rarely, are married couple who are going through conflict holding their emotions. Then, bring in the spiritual aspect of a pastor's work and you have even more emotion. The spiritual person is the most intimate part of an individual and this is the area that pastors tread. When people come to counseling, understanding that emotions are high will help create an atmosphere of cooperation and provide a greater potential for a positive outcome. Unbridled emotions are a danger to growth and progress.

Having people who are understanding and willing to support the pastor during times of conflict is a relief to the pastor. It is essential that church members look for ways to reduce the amount of conflict that their pastor encounter. Whether it be grumbling in the congregation about the worship style, carpet color, a sermon, or knowing that relationships are in turmoil, a pastor relies on others to offer help. Be careful to not assume that the pastor has all the skills necessary to handle every conflict that arises in the church. Remember, that the church is "joined and held together by every joint with which it is equipped, when each part is working properly, makes the body grow so that it builds itself up in love" (Ephesians 4:16, ESV). The pastor equips so the people can work together to grow in love.

Questions to consider:

What are some current tensions you are noticing in your church?

Consider how you can help the pastor deal with those tensions?

Challenge: Pray for the pastor, specifically about conflict.

Encouragement

Encouragement can be defined as *spurring one on to courage*. This definition indicates that there are moments that people need courage. Pastors need courage. Ephesians 6:12 (ESV) explains that "we do not wrestle against flesh and blood, but against the rulers, against the authorities, against the cosmic powers over this present darkness, against the spiritual forces of evil in the heavenly places." This is the space that pastors work in all the time. Pastors have responded to the call to enter into a lifetime of being on the frontlines of spiritual battle. They need to be encouraged.

What a frustrating and exhausting meeting. All Pastor Don was suggesting was a new way to reach the families at the middle school down the street. He wanted to offer after school tutoring once a week and provide snacks for the kids. What he thought would be accepted and supported by the board, turned out to be a fiasco of irritation and frustration. Margaret, a retired schoolteacher, was adamantly against the idea and made it clear that allowing kids into the church. No decision was made, and Margaret left frustrated and questioning her service on the church board.

There are more moments like this than people understand or are willing to admit. Churches are filled with broken people trying to function in a broken world. It would be nice to say that the church provides the escape for conflict and division, however, that is not the case, nor will it ever be. Pastors dwell within the brokenness and try to be a source of strength for all members of the church. This task is unreasonable and should not be expected.

As Pastor Don walked dejected to his car, Roy, Janice, and Howard met Don at his car. They wanted to pray with him and assure him that they did not share the opinion of Margaret. They also wanted to appreciate Don for having vision for the community and the willingness to use the church building to reach the youth. Though their words did not solve the conflict, it did encourage Don and give him strength to carry on.

There are countless moments of conflict in the church. For instance, church members will worship together on a Sunday morning and then immediately after be arguing over where the dumpster should be placed in the parking lot in a business meeting following service. Another example is a member who paid for the carpeting in the nursery being upset that the room needed to be used for a growing youth group. Regardless of the reasons for conflict, no pastor delights in tensions between themselves and church members. Since conflict is inevitable, pastors need to know they are not alone. Telling the pastor that you are on their side and understanding the impacts of conflict on the pastor is encouraging to the pastor.

Questions to consider:

What ways have you participated in conflict with pastor or other church members?

Where do you see conflict currently occurring in the church?

Challenge: Take the time to encourage your pastor this week. Be creative and have fun!

CHAPTER 5:

AUTONOMY

(BEING ALONE IS GREAT!)

What does it mean to be autonomous? Are pastors controlled by their churches or do they have unilateral ability to make decisions? There are different structures of church polity, most pastors are held accountable to a church board or congregation. This can cause hesitation for some pastors to make decisions on their own. Yet, the ministry demands moments when a pastor can confidently make a decision without consulting the board or the congregation. Autonomy helps a person feel personally secure, have confidence, and regulate their personal behavior.

Decision Making

The birds were singing, and Pastor Don looked out his office window. He was feeling a little bit refreshed but still feeling insecure in who he was and his ability to fulfill his role at the church. Just then, he recalled a moment that happened two years ago. The youth minister had approached him about an opportunity to serve a mission project. This project required packing 40,000 dry good meals for a regional organization. It also cost $.25 per meal. The decision needed to be made before the next congregational meeting. Don took a risk and agreed to commit the church to the project. The next Sunday, Don appealed to the congregation to participate and to sponsor the meals. Within two days, they had the $10,000 needed for the project and nearly 60% of the church had volunteered to help. Additionally, Mark received many excited compliments for the project and the youth minister received accolades as well.

There are few decisions that pastors make that do not impact church members. This creates a daunting and apprehensive environment. When a pastor feels a sense of autonomy that gives them the freedom that they are valued, and they have greater confidence to move the church forward. *The Common English Bible* translates Proverbs 29:18a to say, "when there's no vision, the people get out of control" and part of the pastor's job is to cast vision. If a pastor does not feel they are empowered to make decisions, vision will be limited, and the church will suffocate. Be warned: It is not good for all the decisions to be the pastor's sole responsibility either. Pastors need to know that they can make decisions and that church members will support them.

Questions to consider:

What decisions do you expect your pastor to make without consulting the congregation?

Why should the pastor need congregational approval or board approval for decisions?

Challenge: Tell the pastor how you support the vision for the church. If you are unsure what the vision is, ask the pastor what their goals for the church are and how they want to impact the community.

Ability to Do the Job

No pastor wants to suck at their job. When pastors get together, they measure one another by church attendance and how many activities are offered to church members throughout the week. Few books for pastors are written by guys who served a thirty-person church for over twenty years. This creates a pressure on pastors to strive for numbers. Listen; numbers are important, but they are not the goal. The goal is disciple-making. Pastors want to know that people are growing in their relationship with the Lord. They want to know that their efforts are actually impacting people's lives for eternity. Pastors want to know that they are helping church members live the Christian life.

Pastor Don began to smirk as the Holy Spirit continued to remind him of moment after moment where Don felt affirmed and successful in his work. Agnes was frustrated because she was not able to attend church anymore. Health complications and her propensity to fall had her home-bound. She called Pastor Don and told him how depressed she was feeling because she was unable to attend service and be with her church family. Don researched and presented a plan to the council to begin live streaming the services.

The council approved the idea and thanked Pastor Don for thinking of streaming. Once everything was set up, he went over to visit Agnes and set her computer up so that she could join the services from home. Agnes cried and thanked Don for caring and for making a way for her to participate in the services. She also thanked him for his preaching.

To know that people are appreciative of your efforts makes a pastor feel good about his ability to accomplish his calling. They need to know that they are successfully doing their job. Often, pastors discover the feeling of doing their job outside of the normal Sunday morning church activity. The greatest moments of ministry impact come outside of normal church activity. It is in the intimate moments of life, when church members express that they are feeling cared for and that the pastor is positively helping them in their faith walk, pastors feel accomplished in their calling.

The relationship that Pastor Don had with Agnes actually started years before. Agnes had come back to church after being away for over sixty years. She was raised in the church but left the church when she turned eighteen. She had no need for God or for the perceived burden that she experienced in the church growing up. Agnes walked in the doors of the church four years after her husband passed away. She was desperate and feeling like there was a great void in her life. She was seventy-eight years old and began looking at the Bible with fresh eyes. She attended Bible study faithfully and asked questions, not just in class, but throughout the week. She had been at the church for about a year, and she asked Pastor Don to baptize her. When she asked him, she explained that Don helped her understand the beauty of Christ all throughout the Bible and thanked him for his patience in explaining tough concepts recorded in the Bible.

What relief it is to know that people are actually receiving instruction from the pastor. Pastors desire to be effective in helping people understand how the Bible relates to their daily lives. When pastors spend time educating themselves, they do it for others. It is valuable to pastors to know that they are doing their job and doing it well. The job of the pastor is more than a few cute words on Sunday mornings. Their job is every moment of every day, with the intention of being a benefit to church members. When they know they are doing their job, they are encouraged and build up to continue on.

Questions to consider:

How is your pastor doing their job well?

What ways can you help the pastor accomplish their calling or job?

Challenge: Tell the pastor how they are helping your faith grow.

CHAPTER 6:

PROBLEM SOLVING/SELF-ACTUALIZATION

(I CAN FIX IT)

Problem Solving/Self-Actualization focus on one's ability to make decisions. This ability includes how well a person analyzes situations and circumstances, the way in which they adapt to change, and one's thoughts and feelings on growth and personal development. Many churches value education and most church members expect their pastors to have a level of competence that comes from immersion in study. Some denominations have standard educational requirements for a person to hold the position of pastor. Additionally, most churches encourage pastors to attend conferences, seminars, and continuing education.

Supports Growth and Development

There was a gentle breeze over the Sea of Galilee. The boat that Pastor Don in softly swayed back and forth. Don took a deep breath as he remembered the momentous experience years ago. No course in a classroom could have ever taught him what he learned in those nine days walking the very places that Jesus walked. He had long wanted to go to Israel but had never been able to afford the trip. He was sharing at a church barbecue with some members this desire. Three weeks later a couple arrived at his office on a Tuesday (Tuesdays are weird days…not Monday, not Friday Eve, and not Hump Day). They explained to Don that they wanted to bless him and send him on a trip to Israel. All expenses paid. What an amazing gesture!

Not every church has members that can send their pastor to Israel. Every church does have church members that can be attentive to the simple ways a pastor desires to grow and develop. Pastors long to bring value and inspire others to grow through study and experience. Life learning is often the mantra of the Christian. This is especially true for pastors. They learn and study to inspire others to learn, grow, and study.

PROBLEM SOLVING/SELF-ACTUALIZATION

Sam noticed a line item missing in the proposed church budget. It was Pastor Don's first year at the church. He was young, excited, and inexperienced. Though Don had been to seminary, his practical experience was limited. "What about continuing education?" asked Sam. The congregation sat silent. Dr. Clay was a professor of anthropology at the local state university and began to speak. He supported the fact that it was important to invest in Pastor Don's continuing development. "What makes pastor better, makes the church better." Dr. Clay explained. The line item was added and has been a staple in the budget ever since.

It is essential that pastors grow. We desire pastors to grow spiritual, but we should also desire that they grow in their ability and knowledge. Too often, church members do not consider the continuing education needs of the pastor. Major companies spend millions of dollars giving their management continuing education. Other professions require continuing education to maintain certifications and certificates. Churches should look for ways to encourage and support the pastor in their growth and development.

Questions to consider:

Does your church have a line item in the budget for the pastor's continued growth?

What conferences or seminars does your pastor attend?

Challenge: Ask the pastor if there are any books or seminars they would like to have or attend. Then look for ways to provide that for them.

Values Opinion

Pastors are in the helping profession. They share advice and are asked to counsel church members about all aspects of life. However, one of the challenges many pastors face are church members valuing their opinion and their experience outside of the ministry. Many pastors have had careers previous to going into the ministry. Some pastors have balanced the demands of the ministry while holding a full-time job. The experiences that pastors bring can be extremely valuable.

Six years ago, the church needed to expand the sanctuary to accommodate increased attendance. Pastor Don listened as board members discussed and disagreed about how to move forward. Eventually, the board asked Don his opinion. Don had been in construction management for ten years before he responded to the call of ministry. At the request of the board, Pastor Don was able to add valuable input and save the church money. The addition was seamless and accomplished the additional space needed.

There are many times that a pastor's experiences outside of the church are discounted. In fact, often pastors are not consulted about decisions that they were previously experts. This does not mean that a pastor has the answer for everything, but they do offer a perspective that has learned to view life's decisions from a Christian worldview. An outside opinion, especially a godly opinion, is valuable.

Five years ago, Greg pulled Pastor Don aside after service. Greg was a successful businessman who had been in pharmaceutical sales. Greg had been offered a regional position with another medical company, and he wanted Don's thoughts. "Let me take you to lunch this week, Pastor." Greg suggested. On Tuesday afternoon, the two sat down and Greg explained his new opportunity. Don listened and was quiet. "Well, Pastor, what should I do?" Greg asked. Don took the time to share his thoughts and help Greg process the pros and cons. The lunch was ended with Don praying for Greg to receive wisdom from God for the future.

Opinions are plentiful. Not all opinions are helpful. Pastors long to share life with church members and want to feel they add value to others. When church members ask for advice from pastors concerning life and matters outside the church, pastors feel validated and more confident in their ability to serve others. (After all, pastors have the best opinions on all things☺). Though this might sound narcissistic, the motivation for a pastor to share their opinion with church members stems from wanting to share life with church members. Sermons are the gateway to real life conversations between pastor and parishioner. After all, pastors are not greater than the church member, they are simply doing their part in the body as the Spirit sees fit.

Questions to consider:

When have you thought the advice of the pastor would be beneficial?

Do you find that you separate the spiritual matters of life from the normal everyday life? If so, note the areas that you have considered non-spiritual in your life?

(*Understand: There is no separation between the Christian life and normal life.)

Challenge: Take the time to thank your pastor for the advice they gave. Be specific and explain how it impacted your life.

CHAPTER 7:

INTERPERSONAL RELATIONSHIP SKILLS

(LET'S JUST BE FRIENDS)

Who doesn't want to be liked? Of course, we want to be liked and share our lives with people we get along with. Pastors are no exception. Most pastors want to be liked and they desire to have friendships with everyone. It's true; pastors want to be friends with you. Have you ever thought that you could be friends with your pastor? This means more than a friend on Sunday or a friend that knows more stuff about God than you. A friend that you laugh with, share life with, cry with, go on trips with, hang out at barbecues with, get real with.

Interpersonal Relationship Skills speaks to one's ability to give emotional support to others, maintain close personal relationships, establish interpersonal relationships, and empathize with the feelings of others. Interpersonal Relationship Skills addresses the aptitude to establish friendships that are lasting with others. It also addresses how one understands the feelings of others and can give emotional support. These questions addressed how church members have helped pastors maintain close friendships that extended beyond the pastor/parishioner boundaries. Much warning has come to the pastors about having church members as friends. This philosophy has caused a separation between pastor and church member, often leaving the pastor feel isolated and alone. Most seminaries, ministry books and advice tell pastors that they cannot be friends with church members. Remember, pastors are people and people are relational. They really want to be friends.

A notification rang on Pastor Don's phone. It was a reminder of his tee time with Hal, James, and Shawn. The four began golfing together shortly after Don arrived as the new pastor. Don remembered his second Sunday he was connecting with people as they exited the service after church. Hal was wearing a "Titleist" polo shirt. Don made a comment about the shirt. Hal stopped and inquired, "Do you play golf?" Don explained that he likes to go from time to time. The next thing Don knew, it was Thursday and Hal was introducing him to James and Shawn. James and Shawn rarely came to church, but they golfed with Hal every Thursday. They now had a fourth, Pastor Don.

Common interests connect people. To clarify, not every pastor plays golf (although they should. Another observation, golf is expensive. Pay pastors more so they can play). Whether it be fishing or golf, or needlepoint (well, maybe not), pastors want to hang out around common interests. Do you know what your pastor likes to do outside the church? Are there any common interests that you share with your pastor? There is a perception that pastors always talk about God and that they constantly speak in theology. This is simply not true. Pastors are people, people just like you. They are trying to stay close to Jesus and live a life that glorifies God. Friendship aids in the journey to heaven.

Trust/Confidentiality

It was two years ago, hole four (the dreaded long five par), that Shawn sliced a shot near where Pastor Don had shot. As they were looking for Shawn's golf ball, Shawn asked if he could confide in Don. Of course. Shawn shared how he and his wife were struggling and he knew that much of it was his fault. He couldn't seem to not be angry and selfish. Don offered to meet with them. Shawn denied the request but suggested that they should share a cart on golf Thursdays so that they could talk. Don agreed and explained to Shawn that he wanted to be a friend that walked alongside him and that he didn't do any counseling on the golf course. It distracted him from his mediocre ability to play the game. A year later, Shawn and his wife were doing well, expecting their first child, and attending church. On hole four (the dreaded long five par), Shawn thanked Don. For what? He thanked Don for being trustworthy and keeping what he shared about his struggles confidential.

Pastors should be safe confidants. Yet, if church members do not spend time with the pastor, they cannot share as openly as friends do. Some of it stems from the fact that people feel conviction when the pastor is present. It's weird, but true. When people spend time with pastors outside of church, real life conversations can occur, and real friendship can blossom. It is important to note, that pastors understand that they are called to be a place of safety for people to share their deepest secrets. When people spend time, socially, with their pastor, the discover that they are trustworthy and gracious. Pastors protect the conversations they have with church members, because they are friends and the want to protect the relationship.

INTERPERSONAL RELATIONSHIP SKILLS

Questions to consider:

Do you feel comfortable enough to be vulnerable with your pastor? If not, why not?

When has your pastor shown that they are trustworthy?

Challenge: Ask you pastor what they life to do outside of church. Discover a common interest and plan a way to share that interest together. (It means you might have to pay ☺).

Share Life and Stories

Everybody has a life, and everybody has a story. Life is enhanced when it is shared with others and when stories are created with others. Pastors long to invest in the lives of others. They enjoy hanging out and creating memories. Consider the moments you have shared with your pastor. Maybe there were moments that occurred during a trial or a tragedy. It could have been a moment of great joy. Pastors are often invited into the most intimate moments of a person's life. The death of a loved one, the joy of marriage, the diagnosis of cancer, the excitement of a newborn, are all moments that are shared with a pastor. These are moments in life that can be catalysts for a deeper friendship with the pastor.

Dust was flying everywhere, and Don began to cough as he covered his eyes. Mike laughed at Don. It was the first time that Pastor Don had been on a tractor in the midwest during harvest. Let's be honest, it was the first time Don had been on a tractor, … ever. Mike jumped at the chance to share his life as a farmer with Don. He had admitted that he thought it would be funny to get Don out on the farm. Once the dust settled, Mike and Don sat for two hours and just talked about their lives. Don recalled what an unusual but wonderful moment that first tractor ride was. It was the first of many. Mike was a third-generation farmer and he loved it. He enjoyed being out in the field and he enjoyed sharing his life with Don. Tractor rides turned into weekly lunches, yearly birthday celebrations, and Don learning how to make homemade root beer.

Life is enriched when it is shared with others. Shared experiences connect people in a way that cannot happen at a Sunday morning church service. Pastors enjoy spending time with people and actually find great joy in spending time with them. In fact, pastors discover an increased ability to speak into the lives of church members when they know them as friends. General advice is easy, but often misses. Connection breeds context and lives shared births meaning.

"Pastor Don, you're coming to our 4th of July party, and I won't take no for an answer." Claudia stated assertively. Don clarified that his wife was included in the invitation and what they could bring. Don and Deborah arrived that Saturday at the community park. Claudia shouted, "Over here!" It was clear that Don and Deborah were the only "non-family members" at the party. Claudia introduced them to each person in her family. This began a long relationship that included every Christmas Eve, Memorial Day, Labor Day, Thanksgiving, …any birthday or reason for celebration. Pastor Don remembered Claudia's family members one by one begin to attend church. He remembered baptizing kids, cousins, aunts, uncles, and kids. He shared in the joy of new members marrying into the family and grieved greatly when Grandpa Jim passed away. Don and Deborah were part of the family.

There is great fulfillment in sharing life with others. Pastors desire to be included in the special moments of people's lives. They want to be part of your family. Though a pastor my marry and bury, it brings greater meaning when they know the family. This happens when pastors are included in the normal activities of life. Now, not every pastor is going to connect or click with your family, but this does not mean that you cannot share life with them.

Questions to consider:

What ways have you included your pastor in your life?

Why do you hesitate to ask your pastor to partici-pate in normal moments in your life?

Challenge: Invite your pastor to hang out and share the story of your life. Consider explaining; where you were born, what you do for a living, what you like about your town, why you come to the church, etc...

Invitation to Socialize

When pastors are invited to someone's house, they get excited, and they get nervous. Why are they nervous? Well, they first wonder, "why am I being invited over"? Over and over again, pastors are invited to someone's house only to enter into an agenda driven evening. Church members want to influence and share their opinions about how the pastor should proceed with the ministry. Gossip about the other members of the church is present and tension fills the room. You can understand why pastors get a bit apprehensive when they are invited over.

His phone vibrated informing him that he had a text. Don looked and noticed that it was from Paul. Paul was confirming that Don and Deborah were still planning to go camping next week with them. Don remembered the first time Paul invited him over. With hesitation (not visible to Paul), Don agreed. As they pulled into Paul's driveway, Don and Deborah said a quick prayer that God would bless their time. Paul and Jan welcomed them in with great smiles and open arms. As they sat in the living room, Paul began "Don, I wanted to have you over to let you know" (*oh boy, here it comes*, Don thought) "how blessed we are

84

to have you here. We want you to relax and enjoy our times together." Times? Was there more than just this once? Paul continued to express his understanding of how Don and Deborah carry the weight of the church. He and Jan just wanted to get to know them and give them a safe place to relax. The evening was filled with laughter and shared moments from the past as the told of their lives.

It is necessary for pastors to unwind. It is needed. Pastors need to know that people care about them as a person and not only someone who has spiritual advice and counsel. When a church member invests in the pastor personally, pastors feel the freedom to be themselves and this will transfer to their approach to others.

Pastor Don recognized that the first night at Paul and Jan's was wonderful. It seemed too good to be true. Jan and Deborah hit it off and none of them wanted the night to end. As Don and Deborah drove home that evening, they were amazed and refreshed that people were genuinely interested in them. The next day Paul texted Don to let him know how much they enjoyed their evening and that he couldn't wait to get together again. This friendship was built upon subsequent invites. Paul and Jan continued to invite Don and Deborah to share life. They would go to ball games, movies, and day excursions together. They would watch each other's dogs. Life was better because of their friendship. It was better because they were invited to come over.

Being invited over is great, being invited subsequent times is better. Pastors want to be friends with everyone, and they really find great joy in spending time with church members. In fact, often their messages can have a greater impact because they share life with church members and can speak appropriately to the congregation. However, pastors can't possibly host everyone. They need church members to invite them to socialize.

Questions to consider:

Have you invited the pastor to socialize? If not, why not?

If you have invited the pastor to socialize, has it been more than once?

Challenge: Invite the pastor to socialize. Don't wait. Make it happen within the next two weeks.

CHAPTER 8:

AFFIRMED ONCE AGAIN

Don stood up and stretched. He exhaled and chuckled a bit. God was good. God had met him in his moment of despair and reminded him how greatly he has been loved by the people in his congregation. He remembered his calling and was convinced the Spirit was affirming his calling through the members of the church. Over and over again, God flooded his memories of the joys of investing in the loves of people. Don could carry on and once again felt excited to serve as pastor. Don made a note in his calendar and set a reminder: "Remember those that love me".

Though pastors agree that they have received a holy calling from God to serve the church, the calling is only as good as the affirmation they receive from the church. The Apostle Paul recalled his desire to visit the church in Rome and prayed "that I may be delivered from the unbelievers in Judea, and that my service for Jerusalem may be acceptable to the saints, so that by God's will I may come to you with joy and be refreshed in your company" (Romans 15:31-32, ESV). Being together, sharing life, refreshes the Spirit. God is relational and being made in his image makes us relational too.

We see in many instances that people are meant to minister the gifts of God to one another and build them up in love. The pastor is no exception. 1 Corinthians 16:17-19 (ESV), the Apostle Paul states, "I rejoice at the coming of Stephanas and Fortunatus and Achaicus, because they have made up for your absence, for they refreshed my spirit as well as yours. Give recognition to such people." Paul, the great missionary of the church needed refreshment. If Paul needed refreshment, so do pastors.

Personal Note

I wanted to take a moment and share why I think this topic of pastor positive mental health is so essential to church success. I have grown up in the church. I have served in differing pastoral roles over the years. I noticed that many pastors feel alone and isolated. Now, understand this is often due to their own narcissistic and paranoia tendencies. Yet, church members come to church and just assume that this is the way the church is set up. Wrong!

This isolation gives the impression that pastors are somehow above the church members. I mean we erect elevated stages and lofty pulpits that could cause that conclusion. Pastors are in a position that creates a level of continually giving. They give advice. They give the word of God. They always have to pray at gatherings (or people assume they do). The list grows and grows. Church members can feel intimidated by their interactions with the pastor because the pastor appears to have it all together (many times this is the reason pastors don't want people to get to know them). All in all, the structure that is common between pastor and parishioner is flawed, broken, and destructive.

I know that these are harsh words. They are not intended to be harsh but to create an awareness of the need. Pastors need friends. You need friends. Pastors need to be affirmed. You need to be affirmed. Isn't it satisfying when you receive feedback from someone that is positive? Of course! Pastors are no different than you. Seriously, they aren't. They are fragile and broken just like the rest of us and in desperate need for Jesus to continually work. My hope is that we would take the charge to care for our pastors as we would a loved one. We would love one another, including our pastor, well.

AFFIRMED

May God richly bless you. Enjoy Jesus! Go and share life…with your pastor.

REFERENCES

10 facts on mental health. (2019). World Health Organization. https://www.who.int/news-room/facts-in-pictures/detail/mental-health

Adams, C. J., Hough, H., Proeschold-Bell, R. J., Yao, J., & Kolkin, M. (2017). *Clergy burnout: A comparison study with other helping professions.* Pastoral Psychology, 66(2), 147-175. doi:10.1007%2Fs11089-016-0722-4

Cowen, E. L. & Kilmer, R. P. (2002). *Positive psychology: Some plusses and some open issues.* Journal of Community Psychology, 30(4): 449–460. doi:10.1002/jcop.10014

Engelberg, J., Fisman, R., Hartzell, J. C., & Parsons, C. A. (2016). *Human capital and the supply of religion.* Review of Economics & Statistics, 98(3), 415-427. doi:10.1162/REST_a_00582

Francis, L., Laycock, P., & Brewster, C. (2017). *Work-related psychological wellbeing: Testing the balanced affect model among Anglican clergy*. Religions, 8(7), 1-11. doi:10.3390/rel8070118

Francis, L. J., Village, A., Bruce, D., & Woolever, C. (2015). *Testing the balanced affect model of clergy work-related psychological health: Drawing on the US congregational life survey*. Research in the Social Scientific Study of Religion Vol, 26, 237-249. doi:10.1163/9789004299436_016

Francis, L. J., & Crea, G. (2018). *Happiness matters: Exploring the linkages between personality, personal happiness, and work-related psychological health among priests and sisters in Italy*. Pastoral Psychology, 67(1), 17-32. doi:10.1007/s11089-017-0791- z

Lau, B. (2018). *Mental health among Norwegian priests: associations with effort–reward imbalance and overcommitment. International archives of occupational and environmental health*, 91(1), 81-89. doi:10.1007/s00420-017-1256-5

Lluch, M. T. (1999) *Construction of a scale for evaluating positive mental health*. (Dissertation. University of

Barcelona, Barcelona).

Lluch-Canut, T., Puig-Llobet, M., Sánchez-Ortega, A., Roldán-Merino, J., & Ferré-Grau, C. (2013). *Assessing positive mental health in people with chronic physical health problems: correlations with socio-demographic variables and physical health status.* BMC Public Health, 13(1), 1–11. doi:10.1186/1471-2458-13-928

MacIlvaine III, W. R., Stewart, W. C., & Barfoot, D. S. (2016). *A biblical theology and pastor survey on local church leadership.* Journal of Ministry & Theology, 20(2), 125–143. https://teleiosresearch.com/dts1-pr/

Maslach, C., Jackson, S. E., Leiter, M. P., Schaufeli, W. B., & Schwab, R. L. (1986). *Maslach Burnout Inventory.* Palo Alto, CA: Consulting Psychologists Press.

Maxwell, J. (2019, August 11). *Why Pastors Leave the Ministry.* Shepherds Watchmen. https://shepherdswatchmen.com/browse-all-posts/why-pastors-leave-the-ministry/

Miner, M., Bickerton, G., Dowson, M., & Sterland, S. (2015). *Spirituality and work engagement among church leaders.* Mental Health, Religion & Culture, 18(1), 57-71. doi:10.1080/13674676.2014.1003168

Portoghese, I., Leiter, M. P., Maslach, C., Galletta, M., Porru, F., D'Aloja, E., ... Campagna, M. (2018*). Measuring burnout among university students: Factorial validity, invariance, and latent profiles of the Italian version of the Maslach Burnout Inventory Student Survey* (MBI-SS). Frontiers in Psychology, 9. doi:10.3389/fpsyg.2018.02105

Proeschold-Bell, R. J., & Byassee, J. (2018). *Faithful and fractured: Responding to the clergy health crisis.* Grand Rapids, MI: Baker Academic.

Proeschold-Bell, R. J., Eisenberg, A., Adams, C., Smith, B., Legrand, S., & Wilk, A. (2016). *The glory of God is a human being fully alive: Predictors of positive versus negative mental health among clergy.* Journal for The Scientific Study of Religion, 54(4), 702-721. doi:10.1111/jssr.12234

REFERENCES

Salwen, E., Underwood, L., Dy-Liacco, G., & Arveson,

    K. (2017). *Self-disclosure and spiritual well-being*

    in pastors seeking professional psychological help.

    Pastoral Psychology, 66(4), 505-521. doi:10.1007/

    s11089-017-0757-1

Vaingankar, J. A., Abdin, E., Chong, S. A., Sambasivam,

    R., Jeyagurunathan, A., Seow, E., ... Subramaniam,

    M. (2016). *Psychometric properties of the positive*

    mental health instrument among people with mental

    disorders: a cross-sectional study. Health and quality

    of life outcomes, 14(1), 1-13. doi:10.1186/s12955-

    016-0424-8

REFERENCES